ON THE WATER

Rowing

by Rachel Grack

BLASTOFF! READERS 2

BLASTOFF! READERS, AN IMPRINT OF BELLWETHER MEDIA BY FLUTTERBEE

Blastoff! Readers are carefully developed by literacy experts to build reading stamina and move students toward fluency by combining standards-based content with developmentally appropriate text.

Level 1 provides the most support through repetition of high-frequency words, light text, predictable sentence patterns, and strong visual support.

Level 2 offers early readers a bit more challenge through varied sentences, increased text load, and text-supportive special features.

Level 3 advances early-fluent readers toward fluency through increased text load, less reliance on photos, advancing concepts, longer sentences, and more complex special features.

★ Blastoff! Universe

This edition first published in 2027 by Bellwether Media, Inc.

For information regarding permission, write to Bellwether Media, Inc., Attention: Permissions Department, 3500 American Blvd W, Suite 150, Bloomington, MN 55431.

Library of Congress Cataloging-in-Publication Data

Names: Koestler-Grack, Rachel A., 1973- author
Title: Rowing / by Rachel Grack.
Description: Minneapolis, Minnesota : Bellwether Media, Inc, [2027] | Series: On the water | Includes bibliographical references and index. | Audience: Ages 5-8 | Audience: Grades 2-3 | Summary: "Relevant images match informative text in this introduction to rowing. Intended for students in kindergarten through third grade"–Provided by publisher"
Identifiers: LCCN 2026013811 (print) | LCCN 2026013812 (ebook) | ISBN 9798898800581 (library binding) | ISBN 9798898801823 (ebook)
Subjects: LCSH: Rowing | LCGFT: Juvenile literature
Classification: LCC GV791 .K64 2027 (print) | LCC GV791 (ebook) | DDC 797.12/3-dc23/eng/20260417
LC record available at https://lccn.loc.gov/2026013811
LC ebook record available at https://lccn.loc.gov/2026013812

Editor: Kieran Downs Series Designer: Josh Brink Designer: Laura Sowers

Printed in the United States of America, North Mankato, MN.

Table of Contents

Ready All, Row!

Rowing is a water sport using **shells** and oars. Shells can hold one to eight rowers.

Competitors race mostly on lakes and rivers.

competitors

Top Place to Row

Henley-on-Thames, England, United Kingdom

There are two types of shells. **Sweeps** have single oars with long handles.

In **sculls**, rowers hold an oar in each hand.

Oar handles are **hollow** and lightweight. They have a **blade** on one end.

Oars sit in **oarlocks** on the edge of the shell.

Rowers dress for warm or cold weather. They wear tight, breathable clothing.

Seat pads make long races more comfortable.

What Rowers Need

Getting Started Rowing

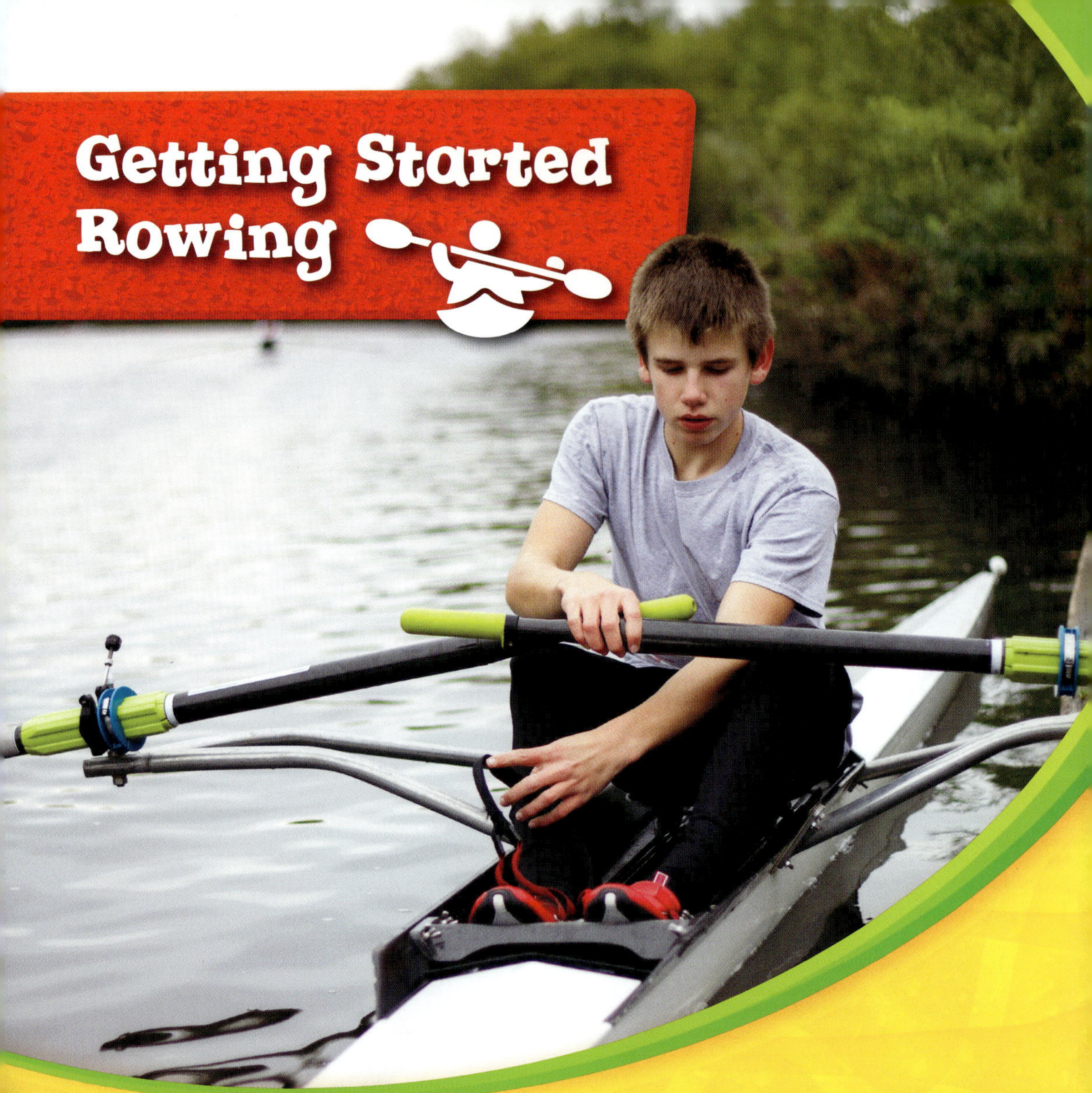

Rowing takes strength and **balance**. Beginners learn rowing on land first.

They practice with rowing machines.

Rowers sit with knees bent. They put their feet in **foot stretchers**.

They hold the oars with their **knuckles** on top.

Rowers put the oar blades in the water. They push with their legs as they pull the oars.

This movement drives the shell forward.

Rowers often race in teams. Teammates all paddle together.

How to Row

They listen to directions from the **coxswain**. The fastest shell wins the race!

Go Race

Rowers must learn to swim before rowing on water. They should always keep a **flotation device** in the shell.

Classes help rowers meet one another. Time to race!

Glossary

balance—the ability to stay upright

blade—a wide, flat surface on an oar

competitors—people who try to win something someone else is also trying to win

coxswain—a person in charge of a rowing shell

flotation device—an object that helps a person float in water

foot stretchers—objects that hold a rower's feet in place

hollow—empty on the inside

knuckles—the round parts of fingers at the ends of two bones

oarlocks—fittings on the edge of a shell that hold oars in place

sculls—rowing boats where the rowers use two oars

shells—long, narrow boats used in rowing races

sweeps—rowing boats where the rowers use a single oar

To Learn More

AT THE LIBRARY

Bolte, Mari. *Rowing*. Mankato, Minn.: Creative Education and Creative Paperbacks, 2024.

Grack, Rachel. *Kayaking*. Minneapolis, Minn.: Bellwether Media, 2027.

Owings, Lisa. *Canoeing*. Minneapolis, Minn.: Bellwether Media, 2023.

ON THE WEB

FACTSURFER

Factsurfer.com gives you a safe, fun way to find more information.

1. Go to www.factsurfer.com.
2. Enter "rowing" into the search box and click 🔍.
3. Select your book cover to see a list of related content.

Index

The images in this book are reproduced through the courtesy of: KOTO, front cover (top); FS Stock, front cover; FS-Stock, p. 3; roibu, p. 4; Anthony Brown, pp. 4-5; Gordon Bell, p. 5; smuki, pp. 6-7; microgen, p. 7; Gianni Caito, p. 8; Raylipscombe, pp. 8-9; WoodyAlec, pp. 10-11; Corvalol, p. 11 (seat pad); MarekPhotoDesign.com, p. 11; SolStock, pp. 12-13, 21; Denis Kabelev, p. 13; soniabonet, p. 14; KOTOIMAGES, pp. 14-15; John Kropewnicki, p. 16; Ivan Smuk, pp. 16-17; David Johnson, pp. 18-19; dmphoto, p. 19 (catch, drive, finish, recovery); YKD, pp. 20-21; Stefan Ugljevarevic, p. 23.